GET TO KNOW
YOUR PET

Cats and Kittens

JINNY JOHNSON

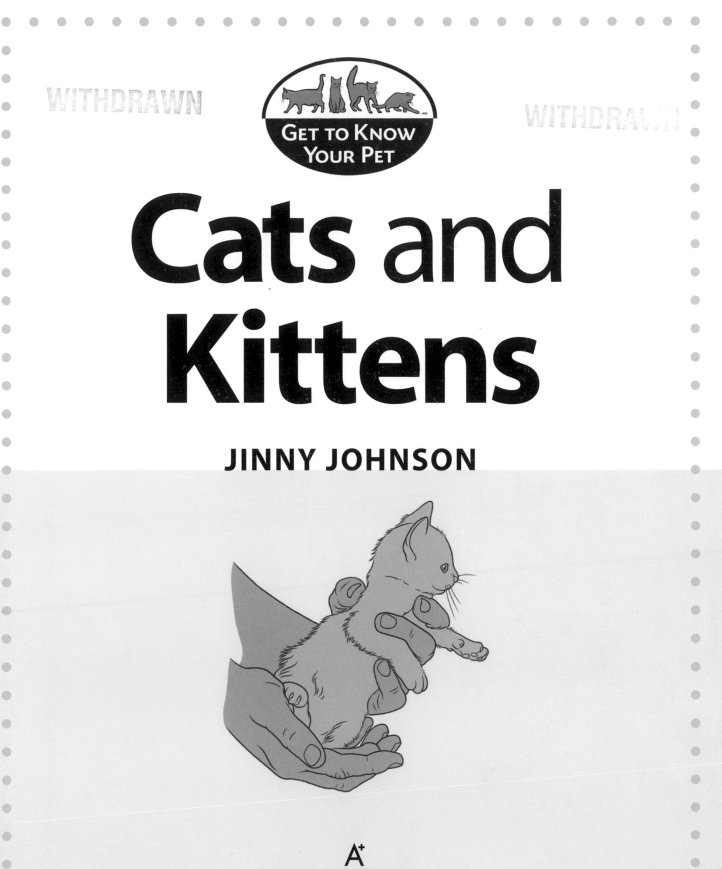

A⁺

Smart Apple Media

Smart Apple Media is published by Black Rabbit Books
P.O. Box 3263, Mankato, Minnesota 56002

Printed in the United States of America

Library of Congress Cataloging-in-Publication Data

Johnson, Jinny.
    Cats and kittens / Jinny Johnson.
    p. cm. — (Smart Apple Media. Get to know your pet)
    Includes index.
    Summary: "Describes the behavior of cats and kittens and how to choose and care for pet cats"—Provided by publisher.
    ISBN 978-1-59920-088-0
    1. Cats—Juvenile literature. 2. Kittens—Juvenile literature. I. Title.
SF445.7.J64 2009
636.8—dc22
                                                        2007043435

Designed by Guy Callaby
Edited by Mary-Jane Wilkins
Illustrations by Bill Donohoe
Picture research by Su Alexander

Thanks to Richard, James, Ella, Simon and Joe
for their help and advice.

Picture acknowledgements
Page 5 Theo Allofs/Corbis; 6 Scott T. Smith/Corbis; 9 Grace/Zefa/ Corbis; 11 Jane Burton/Getty Images; 13 L. Ancheles/Getty Images; 15 & 19 G.K. Hart & Vikki Hart/Getty Images; 20 Daniel Attia/Zefa/ Corbis; 22 Hannah Mentz/Zefa/Corbis; 24 Steve Lyne/Getty Images; 27 (top) Dave King/Getty Images, (bottom) Cath Wadforth/Dept. of Zoology/University of Hull/Science Photo Library
Front cover Walter Hodges/Getty Images

9 8 7 6 5 4 3 2

Contents

Big Cats and Small Cats

Cats make great family pets. They are good company, clean, and lots of fun. They need careful looking after, but they can be left for a time during the day.

Pet cats belong to the same group of animals as lions, tigers, lynxes, and leopards—the cat family. They are often called felines. All cats have very good senses of sight, hearing, smell, and touch. They can sneak up on prey without a sound and run fast for short distances. A cat can also jump up to five times its own height.

4

Cat Characteristics

● All cats walk on their toes, not on the soles of their feet as we do. They have fleshy pads under their toes, which help them walk very quietly.

● A cat holds its claws back in folds of skin called sheaths when it is walking around. This means the claws don't get blunt. The cheetah is the only cat that can't do this.

pads

● Most male and female cats look alike, but a male lion has a big mane of fur around its neck.

● Cats have a very good sense of balance so they can jump and pounce easily.

● All cats eat meat. A cat can't live on plant food.

● Most wild cats (except lions) live and hunt alone.

PET SUBJECT

Q Do pet cats and big cats do the same things?

A Yes, they do. Watch a television show about lions and tigers and you'll see them licking their fur and stretched out asleep just like your cat. Then watch your cat chasing a toy. It will crouch, then pounce like a lion. Your pet cat is a relative of the wild cats, and its behavior can be very similar.

5

A tiger washes by licking its fur and paws in the same way a pet cat does.

FELINE FACT
A cat's skeleton has 244 bones. This is 40 more bones than a human skeleton has.

A Cat's Day

A cat spends half the day asleep. Sometimes it naps with its eyes half-closed, but wakes up if it hears the fridge door open! At other times it sleeps more deeply.

For the rest of the day, a cat sits and watches what's going on, plays, looks for food, and grooms itself. Most cats spend an hour every day licking their fur. A cat that goes outside explores its territory (home area) and may stalk prey—even if it's just a spider.

PET SUBJECT

Q **Why does my cat sleep so much?**

A Wild cats hunt to stay alive, but once they have eaten, they sleep to save energy. The more they move around, the more food they need. A pet cat doesn't need to hunt, but it naturally sleeps a lot. When a kitten sleeps, its body makes a substance called growth hormone that helps it grow.

A Cat's Day

Here's how an adult cat that's allowed outside might spend the day. A kitten would spend more time asleep and playing and would not go outside alone.

Early morning: Sit outside or at the window watching what's going on. Perhaps chase a spider or two.

After breakfast: Groom, then a long nap.

Mid-morning: A little walk around outdoors or inside. Groom again.

Early afternoon: A long nap.

Late afternoon: Outside to check what's happening. Maybe sniff fence posts and mark territory.

Early evening: Groom after supper, then nap or play with toys.

Night-time: Long sleep and maybe some time outside watching what's happening—perhaps hunting a mouse.

GROOMING

A cat cleans itself very carefully. It starts by licking a front paw and wiping it over its face. Then it cleans its front legs and moves onto its back, back legs, tummy, and tail. A cat has a body that can twist and turn to reach almost every part.

Do Cats Talk to Each Other?

Cats may not talk like humans, but they can show how they feel about things. A cat holds its tail, ears, and body in lots of different ways that send messages.

If your cat has a standoff with a neighbor's cat, both will have their ears flat down on their heads. But one will have the ears slightly twisted so that the tips can be seen from the front. This cat is threatening the other one.

PET SUBJECT

Q Why does my cat fluff up its tail when it meets a strange cat?

A It is trying to make itself look as fierce as possible to frighten the other cat. When the fur on a cat's tail stands on end, it makes the cat look bigger. Sometimes the hair on a cat's body stands on end as well.

Tail Telling

Here are some ways your cat can tell you—and other cats—what he's feeling.

● Tail straight up: saying hello to you or another cat.

● Tail straight up and quivering: your cat is nervous and unsure.

● Tail flicking from side to side: your cat may be angry, but could be checking what is behind it.

● Tail with tip curved to one side: the usual tail position and has no special meaning.

● Tail wrapped around body: your cat is happy and contented.

Cats threaten each other by staring, so if you want to make friends with a cat, don't stare. Look at the cat and blink slowly. The cat finds this soothing and friendly.

Smelly Signals

To a cat, smells are like messages that give lots of information about the creature that left the smell.

When a cat pees or poops, it is marking its home territory. Its smell says to other cats, "This is my patch— stay away." Sometimes a cat sprays its pee, which makes the message stronger and more noticeable.

A cat has glands that make an oily, smelly fluid. Most glands are on the face, neck, around its tail, and on its paws. Grooming spreads the smelly fluid all over the body.

When the cat rubs against anything, some of the scent comes off. This helps the cat surround itself with its own smell.

10

A cat's main scent glands are on its face, neck, around its tail, and on the underside of its paws.

Your cat will scratch a tree, a scratching post, or sometimes the sofa! It is sharpening its claws, but it is also spreading its smell from the glands on its paws.

PET SUBJECT

Q **Why does my cat rub his head on my legs when I come home?**

A When a cat rubs against your legs, it puts some of its scent on you. This spreads its smell and makes it feel comfortable and at home. You won't notice the smell, but another cat would.

Cat Chat

Scent messages and tail positions are very useful for talking to other cats. But cats know that humans aren't always good at understanding these signals. So they meow to us more than they do to each other.

Listen carefully to your cat's meow and you'll find it makes quite a few different sounds. Your cat may make a chirping noise to greet you, but a louder meow to remind you that it is suppertime. Cats soon learn that a louder meow is noticed more quickly. You may also hear your cat snarling, hissing, or making a loud yowling sound. It usually does this if it's facing a rival cat or perhaps a scary dog.

A cat knows that meowing is the best way to get your attention, whether it wants supper or just a friendly stroke.

When a cat hisses and holds down its ears, it is saying, "keep away." It may be warning off another cat or an approach by a person it doesn't know.

PET SUBJECT

Q **Why do cats purr?**

A No one knows exactly why and how cats make the deep rumbling sound we call purring. Kittens start to purr when they are only two weeks old, after being fed or groomed by their mom. An adult cat purrs when it is feeling happy. Cats also sometimes purr when they are in pain, perhaps to comfort themselves. Big cats can't purr.

You'll hear your cat purring when it is sitting comfortably on your lap or looking forward to a tasty treat.

Kinds of Cats

There are lots of different kinds of cats. Most pet cats are domestic shorthairs and they are beautiful, friendly animals.

FELINE FACT
There are about 36 different kinds of wild cats. The biggest is the tiger and the smallest is the black-footed cat, which lives in Africa.

Cats may be black, white, black and white, brown, gray, or ginger. Tabbies have striped markings. Pedigree breeds include Siamese, Burmese, and Persians. Some have long hair and they can be harder to care for.

You need to decide whether you want a kitten or an adult cat. Kittens are fun because they are playful and cute, but they need lots of attention and care, especially in the first months. An adult cat will be house-trained and can go outside on its own once it is settled. There are many adult cats in need of a good home.

Short-haired cat

Long-haired cat

One or two?

If you're buying a kitten, you may decide to have two so they can keep each other company. You will have fun watching them play together.

But remember that feeding and caring for two cats costs more. If you have two cats, you may find they spend more time with each other and less with you.

PET SUBJECT

Q **My cat is a year old. What's that in human years?**

A A cat of a year old is about 15 or 16 in human years—it's a teenager. A cat is mature—able to mate and have babies—at about six or seven months old. A five-year-old cat is in its mid-thirties, and a ten-year-old cat is in its mid-fifties in human years. A 16-year-old cat is 80 in human years.

Choosing Your Cat

You can find kittens and cats that need homes at an animal shelter. You will have to buy a pedigree pet from a breeder. Or you could find someone whose pet cat has had kittens, perhaps through the local vet.

Choose a kitten that is lively and interested in what's going on around it. Check whether it is happy near humans and likes being handled. A kitten born into a busy household will be used to people from the start. Kittens and cats from shelters may need time to get used to you. A kitten should not leave its mother until it is eight weeks old.

PET SUBJECT

Q **What are whiskers and why do cats have them?**

A Whiskers are extra-thick hairs that are very sensitive to touch. They help a cat feel its way around and are useful in the dark. They can even sense changes in the air around objects, to help a hunting cat find prey. A cat can bend its whiskers back out of the way when it is eating and hold them forward when it wants to use them.

A healthy kitten will grow into a lively, active cat that will be your companion for many years.

Health Check

When you're choosing a kitten or cat, you and your parents will need to check the following:

Fur: *Make sure it is shiny with no bare patches.*

Eyes: *Should be bright with no weepiness at the corners.*

Ears: *Check that they are clean inside with no dirt or wax.*

Nose: *Should be clean, not runny.*

Under the tail: *There should be no signs of dirty fur or redness.*

Mouth: *Gums should be pink and healthy and teeth white.*

Movement: *Check that the animal moves well and does not limp.*

Breathing: *Check that the animal breathes quietly and doesn't sneeze or sniffle.*

What Your Pet Needs

You don't need to buy much for your cat or kitten. You will need a safe carrier to bring it home in, a litter box and litter, food and water bowls, and perhaps some toys.

You can buy a wicker or plastic carrier at any pet shop. Put some newspaper inside and some soft bedding. If possible, take a piece of bedding from your pet's old home to help it feel safe and happy.

Make sure you wash food bowls every day and replace them if they get chipped or damaged.

You'll need a cat carrier to take your pet to the vet, as well as to bring it home.

Your new kitten or cat will need to stay in at first, so give it a litter box. A kitten will have been shown about litter boxes by its mother so you shouldn't have any problems, but make sure the kitten knows where the litter box is. Put the box somewhere quiet where the cat won't be disturbed.

You might like to make a bed for your new kitten. A cardboard box with some soft material inside will be fine, or you can buy special cat beds. Some older cats sleep in a basket or cat bed, but most cats prefer to find their own sleeping places.

Never disturb your cat when it is in its litter box.

PET SUBJECT

Q **Why does my cat push its paws in and out when it gets on my lap?**

A Cats learn this kneading movement when they are kittens drinking their mother's milk. A kitten pushes its paws into its mother's tummy to make the milk flow from her teats. Perhaps an adult cat does this when it's on its owner's lap to show that it feels happy and at home.

Bringing Your Pet Home

When you bring your new kitten or cat home, how do you think it will feel? A kitten away from its mom and brothers and sisters for the first time will be nervous. Treat it gently and give it time to get used to its new home. It will soon settle down.

Let your pet get used to you before you try to pick it up and cuddle it. Speak softly and be very gentle.

An adult cat will also be anxious about its new home at first and will want to look around and sniff the new smells. Let your kitten or cat get used to one room at a time. If you have another cat or a dog, keep your new cat in a pen for the first few days. Ask your vet about these.

A kitten pen can be useful at first.

Show your new pet its litter box.

Speak very quietly and gently to your new pet. Let it come to you and don't try to grab or hold it. Learn how to stroke your pet quietly and it will soon trust you. Follow your pet's lead. If it seems happy and confident, let it explore more. If it is nervous, keep it in one room for longer.

21

PET SUBJECT

Q **Why does my new kitten go around the house smelling everything?**

A This is your kitten's way of getting used to its new home. It can find out more about a place by smelling than looking. For example, it will be able to tell by smell whether any other cats or pets live in the house. Your home is now the cat's territory, like its home in the wild.

Feeding Your Pet

All cats, from lions to your kitten, are meat-eaters. A cat cannot live on a vegetarian diet. Kittens, like babies, need to be fed small meals often at first.

A kitten between 8 and 12 weeks old needs four or five small meals a day. Gradually give more food in fewer meals. At six months old, your cat should have two meals a day.

Many dried foods are not suitable for very young kittens. Try giving your kitten some dried food and canned food so it can choose which it likes best. Many cats like canned food at mealtimes, but enjoy having some dried food to nibble in between. Everyone thinks cats love milk and some do, but they don't need it. Water is the best drink for cats.

Cats and kittens need a bowl of clean, fresh water to drink from whenever they want.

Types of Food

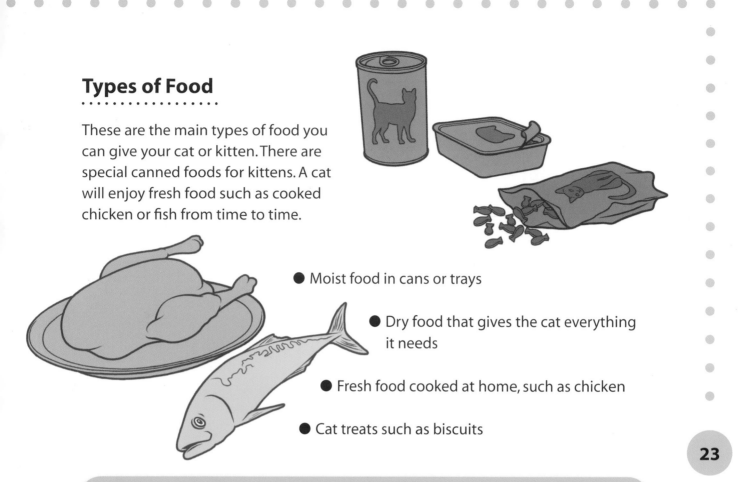

These are the main types of food you can give your cat or kitten. There are special canned foods for kittens. A cat will enjoy fresh food such as cooked chicken or fish from time to time.

● Moist food in cans or trays

● Dry food that gives the cat everything it needs

● Fresh food cooked at home, such as chicken

● Cat treats such as biscuits

PET SUBJECT

Q My cat has plenty to eat. So why does he try to catch birds and mice?

A Cats hunt in the wild, and hunting comes naturally to them whether they need the food or not. When a cat sees a mouse scurrying by or a bird sitting in the garden, it wants to chase it. If it does catch its prey, it may bring it in to share with you. Mother cats do this for their kittens, so your cat may feel it should share with you.

Playtime

Kittens and cats love to play, and playing with your pet is a great way to give it some attention—and have fun yourself.

If you have more than one kitten, they will play together. If you have only one kitten, you'll need to be its playmate. Toy mice, ping-pong balls, and paper bags are all good cat toys. A cardboard box can be great fun—ask an adult to help you make some holes in the sides so your kitten can run in

24

and out. Cats love toys that move, so make a fishing toy. Take a short stick and tie a string on one end. Tie a feather or toy mouse at the other end. Shake this in front of your kitten and it will jump and pounce as it tries to catch it.

Make sure toys are safe for your pet. Don't let it have anything sharp that has corners or that could break in its mouth. String can be dangerous for cats if swallowed, so string is not a good toy.

Kittens love to play, and so do grown-up cats.

PET SUBJECT

Q **Do young cats play together in the wild?**

A They do, and it is important for young cats, such as lion and tiger cubs, to play. As they pounce on leaves and on each other's tails, they are practicing the hunting skills they will need as they grow up. Playing helps make them strong and gives them a chance to practice skills such as creeping up quietly on prey. In the wild, a mother cat will bring prey to her kittens for them to try to catch.

Handling and Grooming

Always be gentle and careful when you pick up your pet. Don't try to pick up your kitten or cat by the scruff of its neck—you could hurt it.

Always lift your pet with both hands and be careful to support its weight. Some adult cats love to be held and carried, but others don't, so respect your cat's feelings on this.

Cats look after their own fur, but many enjoy being brushed and combed. A long-haired cat needs regular help with grooming so its fur doesn't become matted and tangled. You can buy special brushes and combs for cats at a pet shop. Never use your own brush or comb on your cat.

To hold your kitten, put one hand under the kitten's chest just behind its front legs. Put your other hand under its hindquarters and back legs to support its weight.

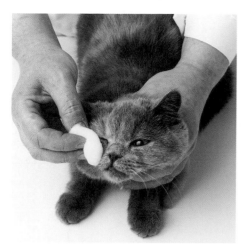

Ask your vet to show you how to wipe away any dirt under your cat's eyes. Use a clean cotton ball moistened with water.

It's a good idea to get your pet used to being brushed and combed while it is still a kitten, particularly if it is a long-haired cat.

PET SUBJECT

Q Why is my cat's tongue so rough?

A The surface of a cat's tongue is covered with lots of tiny spines. They help the cat scrape meat from bones (important for a wild cat). A cat's tongue helps it groom itself; the loose hairs stick to the tongue. A mother cat licks her kittens, and cats that live together lick each other, so your cat may try to lick you!

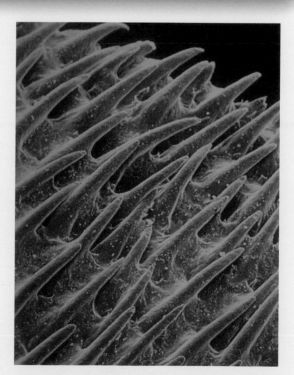

For Parents and Caregivers

Caring for any pet is a big responsibility. Looking after an animal takes time and money, and children cannot do everything themselves. You'll need to show them how to behave around the animal, provide what it needs, and make sure it is healthy and has the necessary vaccinations. You'll also have to neuter the kitten when the time comes and keep an eye on its health.

A kitten may live for 16 years or more, so you're taking on a long commitment. But helping to look after a pet and learning how to respect it and handle it gently is good for children and can be great fun.

CHOOSING A KITTEN OR CAT

Make sure you choose a healthy animal. A kitten raised in a family home will be used to children from the start. An older cat or a kitten from a shelter will need more help to get used to its new home and will take longer to become friendly. Always explain to the person in charge that you want a family pet and ask advice. A cat or kitten from a shelter will have been vaccinated and neutered. When you first get your cat or kitten, take it to the vet for a health check and advice on vaccinations. All cats should be vaccinated against feline infectious enteritis (FIE), cat flu, and feline leukemia virus (FeLV).

Remember that your new pet will need to stay indoors until it is used to its new home. If you let a nervous animal out, it could disappear. A kitten shouldn't go outside until it has had its vaccinations.

LITTER TRAINING

Cats are clean animals and a kitten can usually use a litter box by the time it leaves its mother. Clean out the litter box regularly, and wash and disinfect it thoroughly once a week.

Once your pet is old enough, you can train it to go outside instead of using a litter box. Mix some soil with the litter and move the tray nearer the back door or yard. Tip some used litter from the box on the soil outside. The cat will recognize its smell and get the idea.

FEEDING

You'll need to supervise feeding and buy food, but your child can help, especially if you're feeding dry food. Don't let your child feed your pet many treats or give it human treats such as chocolate. Your child can also help make sure the cat or kitten always has a bowl of fresh water.

HANDLING

It's important to show your child how to handle a cat or kitten properly. If a kitten is handled roughly, it will be nervous and insecure and is unlikely ever to be a loving pet. Teach your child to respect animals and always treat them gently. Don't let them rush up to the kitten and speak loudly, especially at first.

NEUTERING

Pet cats should be neutered to reduce the numbers of unwanted animals. An unneutered male cat is not a suitable indoor pet as he will smell, fight, and wander off in search of mates. An unneutered female will have regular litters of kittens that you'll have to find homes for. Female cats should be neutered by five or six months and males by six or seven months. Ask your vet for advice on this.

Glossary

breeder
Someone who keeps pedigree cats and sells the kittens they produce.

feline
A word used to describe animals of the cat family. It comes from the scientific name of the cat family: *felidae*.

groom
To care for and clean the fur. Cats groom themselves by licking their fur. You can groom your cat by brushing or combing its fur.

growth hormone
A substance produced by the body that helps it grow.

neutering
An operation performed by the vet on a male or female animal so that it cannot have babies. With female animals, it is sometimes called spaying.

pedigree
A pedigree animal is one that is a purebred, such as Siamese or Persian. A pedigree cat has a certificate giving details of its parents.

prey
Animals that are hunted and eaten by other animals.

scent glands
Parts of the body that make a smelly substance used for marking territory.

scruff
The loose skin at the back of a cat's neck.

territory
An animal's home area where it spends most of its time.

vaccination
An injection given to your cat or kitten by the vet to prevent it from catching certain serious illnesses.

Web Sites

For Kids:

ASPCA Animaland: Pet Care

http://www.aspca.org/site/PageServer?pagename=kids_pc_home

The American Society for the Prevention of Cruelty to Animals has some excellent advice about caring for your pets.

Care for Animals: Kid's Corner

http://www.avma.org/careforanimals/kidscorner/default.asp

The American Veterinary Medical Association offers activities and worksheets to help kids be responsible pet owners and find out what they need to know before getting a pet.

Cat Care

http://www.hsus.org/pets/pet_care/cat_care/

The Humane Society of the United States offers cat care essentials, including feeding, communicating, keeping your cat healthy, and much more.

Cat Fanciers' Association: Caring for Cats

http://www.cfainc.org/caring.html

The Cat Fanicers' Association offers advice on pet care and links to information about all the different breeds of pedigree cats.

For Teachers:

Best Friends Animal Society: Humane Education Classroom Resources

http://www.bestfriends.org/atthesanctuary/humaneeducation/classroomresources.cfm

Lesson plans and lots of information about treating animals humanely.

Education World Lesson Plans: Pet Week Lessons for Every Grade

http://www.educationworld.com/a_lesson/lesson/lesson311.shtml

Use the topic of pets to engage your students in math, language arts, life science, and art.

Lesson Plans: Responsible Pet Care

http://www.kindnews.org/teacher_zone/lesson_plans.asp

Lesson plans for grades preschool through sixth, covering language arts, social studies, math, science, and health.

Index